Count Them!
50 Tractor Troubles

A Counting, Spelling and Safety Book

Educational Tractors Series

Book 1

Created by M Larson

M Larson Books

Melanie Larson is a Mom of 3 and farm wife in rural Saskatchewan. Besides creating children's books, Melanie works as an Environmental Consultant in Western Canada. Her other books are called "The Alphabet Construction Troubles", "The Colours in Tractor Troubles" and "The Day I Lost My Bear in Cypress Hills". Melanie and her family stay busy with tractor rides, playing hockey and adventures in Cypress Hills Provincial Park.

www.mlarsonbooks.com

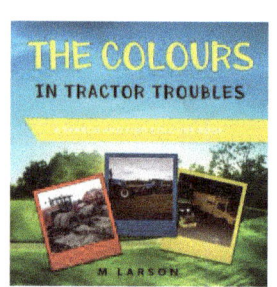
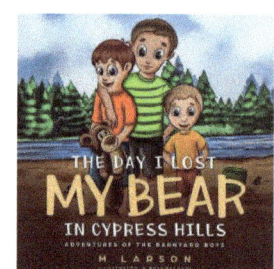

M Larson Books
copyright © M Larson May 2018
ISBN: 978-1-7753218-0-4

All rights reserved.

No part of this publication may be reproduced or stored in a retrieval system, or transmitted in any form or by any means, electronic, mechanical, recording, or otherwise, without written permission of the publisher, M Larson Books, Saskatchewan, Canada. In the case of photocopying, a licence must be obtained from Access Copyright (Canadian Copyright Licensing Agency), 56 Wellesley Street West, Suite 320, Toronto, Ontario M5S 2S3 (1-800-893-5777) or visit www.accesscopyright.ca.

One

Two

Three

Four

Five

Six

7 Seven

8 Eight

9 Nine

10 Ten

11 Eleven

12 Twelve

13 Thirteen

14 Fourteen

15

Fifteen

16

Sixteen

Seventeen

Eighteen

19

Nineteen

20

Twenty

Twenty one

Twenty two

Twenty three

Twenty four

Twenty five

Twenty six

27 Twenty seven

28 Twenty eight

29 Twenty nine

30 Thirty

31 Thirty one

32 Thirty two

Thirty three

Thirty four

35 Thirty five

36 Thirty six

37

Thirty seven

38

Thirty eight

39 Thirty nine

40 Forty

41 Forty one

42 Forty two

Forty three

Forty four

45

Forty five

46

Forty six

Forty seven

Forty eight

49 Forty nine

50 Fifty

Photo Credits:
1. https://i.pinimg.com/736x/6f/66/ef/6f66ef6ac41fc0f232bfbe2decb746db.jpg
2. https://www.facebook.com/FarmingGoneWrong/photos/a.185349961665666.1073741828.18533495   8333833/301991130001548/?type=3&theater
3. https://in.pinterest.com/pin/692921092643755188/
4. https://www.pinterest.capin1113937907631557708autologin=true&lp=true
5. https://i1.wp.com/www.golddustfarms.com/wp-content/uploads/2013/06/2013-John-Deere-Stuck.jpg
6. httpswww.tractorbynet.comforumsfilesattachments606028d1558710162-flail-mower-me-tractor_fail-jpg
7. https://www.facebook.com/FarmingGoneWrong/photos/a.185349961665666.1073741828.185334958333833/375499429317384/?type=3&theater
8. https://in.pinterest.com/pin/692921092643754866/
9. https://in.pinterest.com/pin/692921092643754921/
10. https://in.pinterest.com/pin/692921092643754989/
11. https://www.facebook.com/FarmingGoneWrong/photos/a.185349961665666.1073741828.185334958333833/559886334212025/?type=3&theater
12. https://twitter.com/LynleyWyeth/status/1048836492741603333/photo/1
13. https://www.facebook.com/FarmingGoneWrong/photos/a.185349961665666.1073741828.185334958333833/218581368342525/?type=3&theater
14. https://www.pinterest.ca/pin/330873903848914847/
15. http://uberhumor.com/page/1641
16. https://www.facebook.com/FarmingGoneWrong/photos/a.185349961665666.1073741828.185334958333833/615572015310123/?type=3&theater
17. https://in.pinterest.com/pin/692921092643754963/
18. https://in.pinterest.com/pin/148126275224247237/
19. Contributed by K. Zerr 2017
20. https://www.facebook.com/FarmingGoneWrong/photos/a.185494801651182.1073741829.185334958333833/247834835417178/?type=3&theater
21. http://fox2now.com/2018/01/03/in-deep-trouble-illinois-mans-new-truck-stuck-frozen-after-illegal-four-wheeling/
22. https://www.facebook.com/FarmingGoneWrong/photos/a.185494801651182.1073741829.185334958333833/371971039670223/?type=3&theater
23. https://www.facebook.com/FarmingGoneWrong/photos/a.185349961665666.1073741828.185334958333833/220175941516401/?type=3&theater
24. https://i.pinimg.com/736x/ba/d6/f7/bad6f7e0e58b0fbb0cc0f4c809471012.jpg
25. https://www.facebook.com/FarmingGoneWrong/photos/a.185494801651182.1073741829.185334958333833/347394692127858/?type=3&theater
26. https://www.facebook.com/FarmingGoneWrong/photos/a.185349961665666.1073741828.185334958333833/233048106895851/?type=3&theater
27. https://www.facebook.com/photo.php?fbid=1246520012088545&set=pb.100001916735972.-2207520000.1525807214.&type=3&theater
28. https://i.pinimg.com/236x/1a/e6/63/1ae6634a4b2ed230a044fc0eda37bf2e.jpg
29. https://www.pinterest.ca/pin/399061216962071032/
30. http://tractorsfarmmachinery.blogspot.ca/2013/06/john-deere-accident.html
31. Twitter (@gbowey)
32. https://www.facebook.com/FarmingGoneWrong/photos/a.185349961665666.1073741828.185334958333833/211730112360984/?type=3&theater
33. Contributed by M Zerr 2020
34. https://www.facebook.com/FarmingGoneWrong/photos/a.185349961665666.1073741828.185334958333833/639008696299788/?type=3&theater
35. https://in.pinterest.com/pin/692921092643755178/
36. https://www.pinterest.ca/pin/148126275223428169/
37. https://in.pinterest.com/pin/692921092643754994/
38. https://plus.google.com/u/0/114913029030924336437/posts/TjiqxHzCoNZ?cfem=1
39. https://www.facebook.com/photo.php?fbid=2294750003888283&set=p.2294750003888283&type=3&theater
40. http://i1.ytimg.com/vi/qQfWuoOUWaQ/maxresdefault.jpg
41. https://www.facebook.com/FarmingGoneWrong/photos/a.185494801651182.1073741829.185334958333833/346103922256935/?type=3&theater
42. https://in.pinterest.com/pin/692921092643754733/
43. https://www.facebook.com/FarmingGoneWrong/photos/a.185349961665666.1073741828.185334958333833/593482790852379/?type=3&theater
44. https://www.facebook.com/FarmingGoneWrong/photos/a.185349961665666.1073741828.185334958333833/223970344470294/?type=3&theater
45. https://www.pinterest.ca/pin/574701602419074669/?autologin=true
46. https://www.facebook.com/FarmingGoneWrong/photos/a.185494801651182.1073741829.185334958333833/290700021130659/?type=3&theater
47. https://www.facebook.com/FarmingGoneWrong/photos/a.185349961665666.1073741828.185334958333833/632334720300519/?type=3&theater
48. https://www.agweb.com/article/preventing-an-unwanted-baler-fire--naa-university-news-release/
49. http://www.keywordhungry.com/Y29tYmluZSBhY2NpZGVudHM/
50. https://www.pinterest.ca/pin/459930180678358100/?lp=true

DISCOVER SERIES
INSTRUMENTOS

Llave Allen

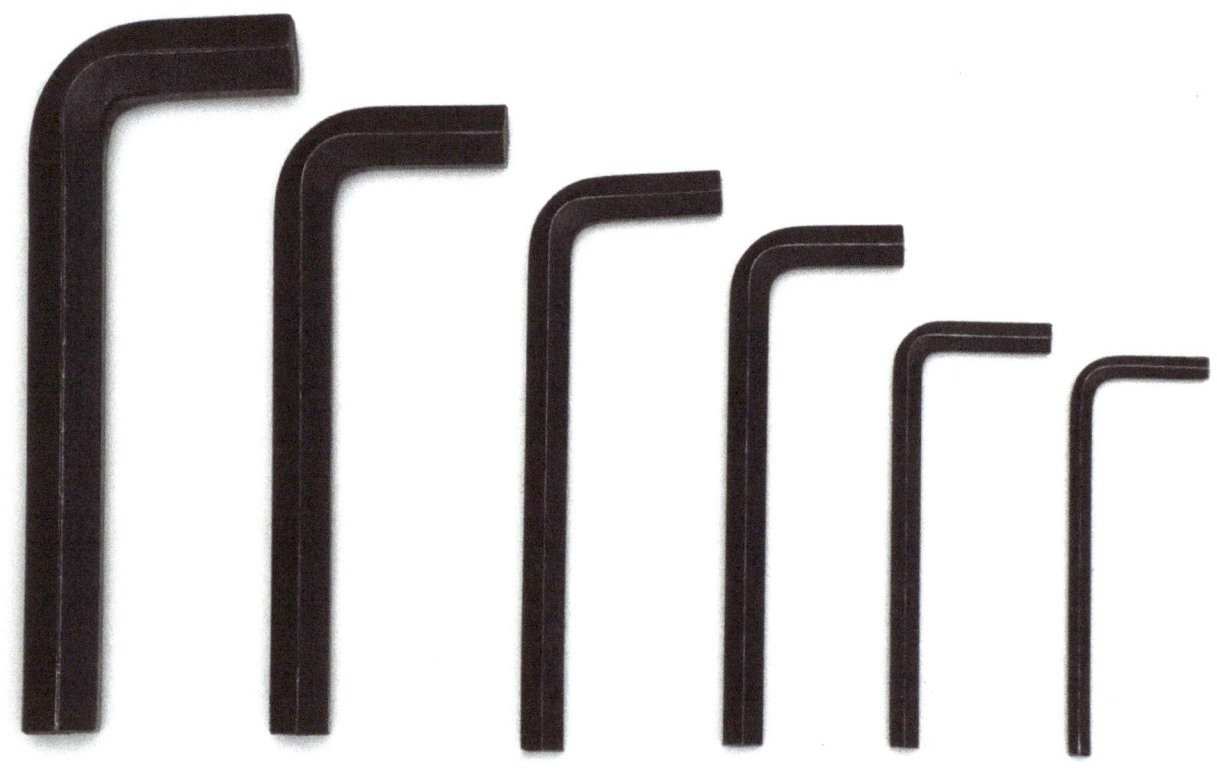

Pistola de Calafateo

Abrazadera